1

Far North Queensland is home to the Yidinji people. Their main town is called Cairns. The Yidinji name for Cairns is **Gimuy** (ghee-moy). This means slippery, blue fig tree. The *Southern Cassowary* lives in the tropical rainforests near Cairns. It is a totem for the Yidinji people and very special to them. They call it **Gindaja** (gin-duh-ja).

Knowledge Books and Software

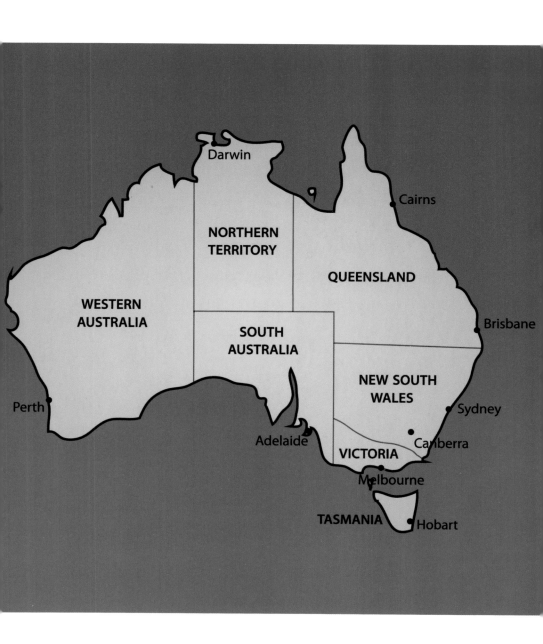

3

In Yidinji story time, Gindaja had large wings and could fly. He lost his way and flew into a very big lake. He got stuck in the mud and flapped his wings but could not free himself. He lost his wing feathers and walked from the lake. The feathers he had left were black from the mud.

Knowledge Books and Software

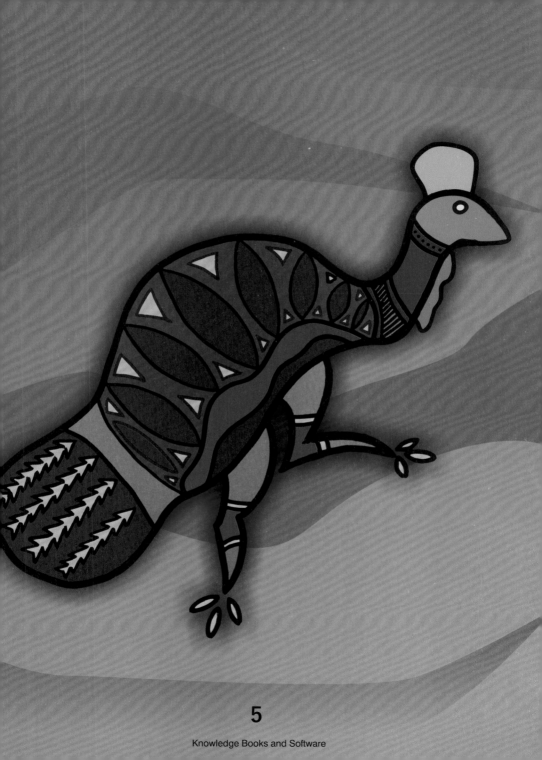

5

Today, the cassowary is a very large bird that cannot fly. It is a bit like an emu. The cassowary is the third tallest living bird in the world. It grows about 2 metres high. Only the ostrich and the emu are taller than the cassowary.

Knowledge Books and Software

7

The feathers of a cassowary are very black and shiny. An adult cassowary has a tall, brown helmet on its head. It also has bright blue, purple and red colours on its neck. Even with all these bright colours, they can still be hard to spot in the rainforest.

Knowledge Books and Software

Adult cassowaries are very strong. They have three toes. The inside toe has a very sharp claw. This is used for scratching in the dirt and fighting other birds. Adult cassowaries also make a deep, rumbling sound. This can mean "stay away!"

Knowledge Books and Software

The cassowary eats over 230 different types of plants and seeds. It is a very important bird for the rainforest. It helps spread the seeds of many trees. This keeps the rainforest strong and healthy. People call the cassowary *"the rainforest gardener"*.

Knowledge Books and Software

Female cassowaries lay up to five large, green eggs. The male cassowary will sit on the eggs for up to 50 days until they hatch. He will also help to raise the chicks until they are old enough to look after themselves.

Knowledge Books and Software

15

Young chicks have striped brown and white feathers. They look very different to their parents! Their feathers change to brown and then black as they grow older. They are adults at 3 years of age.

Knowledge Books and Software

You should never go near cassowaries or their chicks. The adult male will protect them and could hurt you if it feels threatened. They kick with their strong legs and their sharp claws can cause injuries. If you see a cassowary, back away slowly and let it go on its way.

Knowledge Books and Software

19

Cassowary numbers have dropped over the years for many reasons. Some of the land they live on has been cleared for farming and towns. Some have been hit by cars or attacked by wild dogs. Wild pigs can also eat cassowary eggs and destroy their nests. Cyclones have also damaged their habitat, making it hard for them to find food.

Knowledge Books and Software

TAKE CARE

RECENT
CROSSING

Phone 1300 130 372

Queensland

Many things can be done to help the cassowary. Cleared land is being planted with food that cassowaries eat. Councils have put up signs warning people to slow down in cassowary areas. Dogs should be kept on a lead when cassowaries are around. You should never feed cassowaries. You must let them find their own food. All these things can help keep the cassowary safe and healthy for many years to come!

Knowledge Books and Software

Knowledge Books and Software

Word bank

Gindaja

Yidinji

Cairns

Queensland

Southern Cassowary

tropical

rainforests

totem

special

ostrich

helmet

cassowaries

different

important

gardener

protect

threatened

injuries

cyclones

habitat